For Dyan, who saw it first—JB

For Harriet—HJT

Somewhere You Can Dream

Janeen Brian & Hilary Jean Tapper

ALLEN&UNWIN

SYDNEY · MELBOURNE · AUCKLAND · LONDON

Do you love
shadowy secret nooks

or cosy hideaways?

Leafy, shady trees

or sheltered, rocky bays?

Do you love comfy little cubbies

or tree forts
way up tall?

Or spaces behind places

where you can curl up small?

Do you love

snuggling under covers

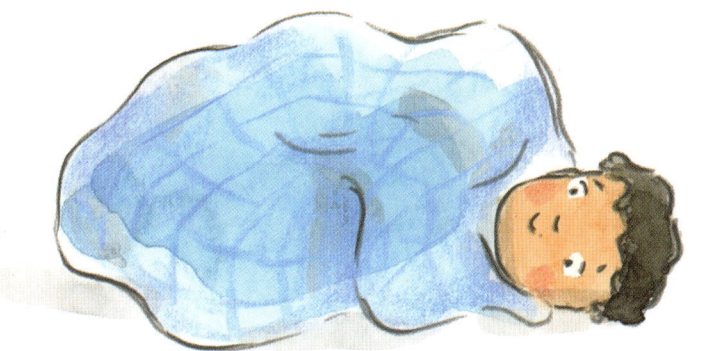

or nestling in a chair

or wriggling
into tiny sites

so you're hardly there?

Or maybe . . .

you love sea and sky

and clouds that are spread out

and hills that roll and valleys deep
that give you room to shout!

But if I had to
make a choice,
I'd choose a
smaller spot

where I could sit,
just me, alone,

and dream and think a lot.

First published by Allen & Unwin in 2026

Allen & Unwin
Cammeraygal Country
83 Alexander Street
Crows Nest NSW 2065
Australia
Phone: (61 2) 8425 0100
Email: info@allenandunwin.com
Web: www.allenandunwin.com

Allen & Unwin acknowledges the Traditional Owners of the Country
on which we live and work. We pay our respects to all
Aboriginal and Torres Strait Islander Elders, past and present.

EU Authorised Representative: Easy Access System Europe, Mustamäe tee 50,
10621 Tallinn, Estonia, gpsr.requests@easproject.com

A catalogue record for this
book is available from the
National Library of Australia

ISBN 978 1 76118 176 4

For teaching resources, explore allenandunwin.com/learn

The illustrations in this book were created using gouache,
watercolour, pencil, ink and crayon.

Cover and text design by Hannah Janzen
Set in 19 pt Baskerville

This book was printed in December 2025 in China by C&C Offset Printing Co. Ltd.

1 3 5 7 9 10 8 6 4 2

janeenbrian.com
hilaryjeantapper.com